The Lion and the Mouse

Written by Anthony Robinson
Illustrated by Ciaran Duffy

Collins

A lion was sleeping.

A mouse was playing.

The lion opened his eyes.

4

He saw the mouse.

6

7

The lion let the mouse go.

8

The mouse saw the lion.

10

He was in a net.

The mouse bit the net.

The lion was free!

A story map

14

ROARʀʀ!

Ideas for reading

Written by Clare Dowdall, PhD
Lecturer and Primary Literacy Consultant

Reading objectives:
- read and understand simple sentences
- use phonic knowledge to decode regular words and read them aloud accurately
- demonstrate understanding when talking with others about what they have read

Communication and language objectives:
- listen to stories, accurately anticipating key events and respond to what they hear with relevant comments, questions or actions
- express themselves effectively, showing awareness of listeners' needs
- develop their own narratives and explanations by connecting ideas or events

Curriculum links: Personal, Social and Emotional Development: Self-confidence and self-esteem; Making relationships

High frequency words: the, is, big, and, can, a, was, he, got, you, me, go, in

Interest words: lion, mouse, sleeping, playing, eyes, saved, free, caught, friends

Resources: paper and pencils

Word count: 68

Build a context for reading

- Ask children to describe when someone was kind to them and how it made them feel.

- Explain that the book is about a lion and a mouse who have to choose whether to be kind to one another.

- Read the title and look at the front cover together. Ask children to describe the animals and say whether they think they will be friends.

- Read the blurb together, pointing to each word as you read. Model how to read aloud with expression.

Understand and apply reading strategies

- Turn to pp2–3. Ask children to read aloud. Discuss how to read longer words, e.g. sleeping, playing. Remind them to use familiar word endings, phonics strategies and the pictures to help them read these words.

- Look at the pictures on pp2–3. Ask children to describe what is happening and to predict what might happen to the mouse.

- Show children the speech bubbles on pp6–7. Discuss the function of the speech bubble and help children to read with different voices for the lion and the mouse.